# Balanced:
# The Little Book of Burnout-Free ERG Leadership

# Balanced:
# The Little Book of Burnout-Free ERG Leadership

Sheryl Miller

Wire Fence Publishing
England, United Kingdom

Copyright © 2024 by Sheryl Miller

Wire Fence Publishing
All rights reserved.

No portion of this book may be reproduced in any form without written permission from the publisher or author, except as permitted by U.K. copyright law.

# Introduction

Being an Employee Resource Group (ERG) leader is one of the most fulfilling roles in any organisation. You are a trailblazer, building communities, making your workplace more inclusive, advocating for others. But let's be honest—sometimes it feels like you're spinning plates - juggling your network responsibilities with your day job. You are doing two jobs, both of them very demanding, and likely only being paid for one.

Burnout is the number one problem that derails networks and leaders. I hear it time and again when I deliver workshops and online sessions. ERG Leaders tell me they feel overwhelmed by workload. If Diversity Equity and Inclusion (DEI) has been deprioritised by senior leadership they also feel like they're fighting a battle. If they don't have an active ERG leadership team or committee they feel like they're doing all of the heavy lifting.

When it comes to spinning plates, the truth is many of the plates only spin when you're actively spinning them. When you turn your attention to something else, they wobble. This constant balancing act can leave you drained, frustrated, and wondering if you're making enough impact. It can also lead to others questioning your level of focus on the day job vs the network.

And here's the thing: ERG leaders are often busy people. They already have big day jobs—many are managers with significant responsibilities. On top of that, they have families, caring responsibilities, and social lives. These are the doers, the go-to people—it's no wonder the saying, "If you want something done, ask a busy person" often applies to them.

I'm writing this book because I want to change that narrative. Over the past few years, I've worked with hundreds of ERG leaders and members, and this book brings together the best of what I've seen. It's designed to help you manage the spinning plates without sacrificing your well-being.

On a personal level, I know how hard it is to juggle everything. I dove headfirst into the world of DEI while researching my first book, Smashing Stereotypes: How to Get Ahead When You're the Only ____ In the Room. I've often struggled to focus, and my passion for making change has sometimes led me to take on too much. Over the years, I've had to work on my own skills of prioritisation, delegation, and self-discipline. This book is me sharing everything I've learned along the way.

As a Chartered Accountant who qualified with EY in the UK, I've led transformation programmes and large workstreams at organisations like National Grid and

Tesco. I've facilitated Boards and Executive teams, worked as a Non-Executive Director, and developed deep insights into change management, senior-level influencing, and organisational culture. This experience has given me a unique perspective on the challenges ERG leaders face and the tools they need to succeed.

This is the one book I feel will help ERG leaders balance the network with the day job, be effective, and have fun while doing it.

Let's turn those spinning plates into a coordinated plan of action—balanced, impactful, and burnout-free.

In this book, I'll share with you my *Ten Commandments* of Balanced ERG Leadership

1. Prioritising: Focus on what truly matters without spreading yourself too thin.
2. Creating a Balanced Plan: Design sustainable initiatives that align with your goals.
3. Delegation: Share responsibilities and empower others to step up.
4. Time Management: Reclaim your schedule and protect your energy.
5. Managing Emotional Labour: Set boundaries and signpost support to protect your well-being.

6. Support Networks: Build relationships that keep you grounded and inspired.
7. Navigating Conflict and Controversy: Handle internal tensions and respond to external challenges.
8. Operating Politically and Strategically: Influence key stakeholders effectively and ethically.
9. Celebrating Wins: Showcase the ERG's achievements and your own contributions.
10. Leveraging External Resources and Communities: Access expertise and collaborate to lighten your workload.

These ten principles will guide you through the challenges and opportunities of ERG leadership.

At the end of each chapter you will find practical steps you can follow to *Create Balance,* as well as *Burnout Busting* tips to keep the feelings of overwhelm at bay.

I also share *Everyday Inspiration* - real life examples of ERG leaders doing big or small things that help to create balance and still have an impact as a network.

Together, we'll create a path to better, fairer workplaces while maintaining a healthy personal and professional balance.

# 1. Prioritising

*"The main thing is to keep the main thing the main thing" Stephen Covey*

As an ERG leader, prioritising effectively is your secret weapon against burnout. With endless possibilities for initiatives, events, and projects, it's tempting to try to do everything. But the reality is, when you spread yourself too thin, nothing gets the attention it deserves. The key is to focus on fewer, high-impact priorities each year.

## The Four-Quarter Rule

Set yourself up for success by selecting one priority per quarter. Think of it as giving yourself the time and space to really nail one big goal before moving to the next. This keeps your workload manageable and ensures balance while driving meaningful results.

# How to Choose Priorities

Start by asking: "What problems is my network trying to solve?" This purpose-led approach will keep you aligned with your ERG's mission. Reflect on the problem your network was originally set up to solve. Many networks, even beyond race and ethnicity networks, were established in response to the 2020 BLM movement and the renewed focus on DEI. What problem(s) were they originally trying to address?

# Data-driven

Next, consider what the data suggests you should be focusing on. Do you have any employee survey data that highlights key issues for members? If not, you may need to rely on anecdotal evidence for now. Begin planning how to gather robust evidence in the future to confirm what the major issues are for your members.

## Create Balance
- Limit your ERG's focus to no more than four priorities per year—one per quarter.
- Align priorities with the problems your ERG was created to solve and validate them with member feedback or data.

- Use tools like this 2x2 matrix to prioritise actions that are high impact and easy to implement.

Prioritisation Matrix

Here's how to use the 2x2 prioritisation matrix with others, for example your committee or the rest of the leadership team. Gather ideas from your team using a silent brainstorm: give everyone 2-3 minutes to jot down ideas. Once you have a list, use a 2x2 matrix to evaluate each idea based on ease (including cost) and impact. Focus on actions that are easy and high-impact while shelving harder or lower-impact ones.

---

## Burnout Busting Tip

Before committing to a priority, ask yourself, "Will this action solve a real problem for my network?" If the answer is yes, you're on the right track.

## *Everyday Inspo: Using Surveys to Define Member Priorities*

*The Co-Chair of the LGBTQ+ Network at a large UK professional body started their New Year planning cycle by designing and running a network member survey. This approach allows the network to go beyond anecdotal evidence and gather direct input from members about their needs, challenges, and priorities.*

*By asking the right questions, the survey provides valuable insights that help the leadership team align their initiatives with what matters most to the members. This data-driven approach not only builds credibility with stakeholders but ensures the network remains relevant and impactful in the coming year.*

## *Key Takeaway:*

*Running a member survey at the start of your planning cycle is a powerful way to confirm your network's priorities and align initiatives with real member needs. It provides a strong foundation for your annual strategy, creating confidence and clarity for both the leadership team and the wider membership.*

Balanced: The Little Book of Burnout-Free ERG Leadership

# 2. Creating a Balanced Plan

*"Balance means doing enough, not doing it all."*

A balanced plan is the secret to leading an ERG sustainably. Without one, it's easy to overcommit and burn out before achieving your goals. By taking a structured approach, you can align your initiatives with your priorities and maintain momentum without exhausting yourself or your team.

Events are highly visible and energising, but the impact can be short-lived and they can be all-consuming from a time perspective, particularly if you don't have enough support to get things done. With the proliferation of awareness days and history months you may even find a level of fatigue setting in such that the impact isn't what it used to be.

On the other hand policy and process change requires time and persistence to implement but these improvements deliver lasting value. Embedding inclusion into policy and process is a core part of impactful, sustainable change.

# The Quarterly Balance

A balanced plan ensures that your network is making a difference both here and now and for the long-term, without overwhelming its leaders and members. The aim is to  a) avoid over-committing and b) strike a balance between one-off events and long-term change.

Each quarter you should have only one main activity or initiative which takes priority. Focus on one of the following elements to achieve both visibility and long-term impact:

## 1. One Event

ERG events typically fall into two categories: flagship events and recurring community-building.

- Hero or Flagship Events: These are your big-ticket events, like International Women's Day or Pride Month celebrations. Flagship events are your ERG's time to shine, creating awareness, engagement, and buy-in. They're also high-risk, high-reward; if they fall flat, they can harm the network's reputation. As such, ERG leaders should focus on overseeing these events to ensure they're impactful and well-executed but make sure there are many hands to spread the load. Ideally these should

be supported by your Internal Communications (Comms) and Events team.
- Recurring Community-Building Events: Examples include lunch-and-learns, fireside chats, book clubs, or Ask Me Anythings (AMAs). These events are great for maintaining member engagement and fostering a sense of community. However, they don't need the same level of leader oversight. Delegate these to committee members or other leadership team members, but ensure there's a standardised, efficient process to prevent burnout of other volunteers.

## 2. One Policy Review

Policies are how change gets embedded within organisations. Your ERG should regularly review existing policies to ensure they align with your inclusion goals. Start by focusing on policies that impact current employees and think broadly across:
- The Employee Lifecycle: Recruitment, onboarding, performance reviews, promotions, and exits.
- Life Stages: Trying, starting, and growing a family; caring for loved ones; dealing with illness, loss, and bereavement.
- The Working Day: Flexibility, hybrid working patterns, and support for the different needs of

the community. Data on preferences for flexible working can also be useful here. For example, it might point to legitimate needs for greater home working or truncated hours. However, be cautious of preferences for home working driven by a desire to avoid the workplace—this might indicate deeper issues, such as feelings of exclusion or an unwelcoming company culture. Redesigning processes to accommodate such preferences without addressing the root causes does not solve the broader problem.

By embedding change into policies, practices, and systems, your ERG ensures its work has a lasting impact.

## 3. One Collaboration

Collaboration amplifies your ERG's reach and impact while sharing the workload. Examples include:
- Partnering with another ERG on shared goals, such as hosting joint events or co-developing training programs.
- Collaborating with internal departments, like Procurement, Sales and Marketing for specific campaigns with suppliers and customers, Leaning & Development (L&D) for leadership

development, Internal Communications for awareness campaigns.
- Engaging with external organisations, such as local community groups, charities, schools, universities, or industry partners, to bring fresh perspectives and resources.

When ERGs look beyond the 'four walls' of their own network, it sends a strong message to senior leaders that the ERG understands it is not a silo. This approach can be a game-changer for securing leadership buy-in and broader company engagement.

## 4. One Process Redesign

Embedding initiatives into Business as Usual (BAU) ensures your ERG's efforts have long-term sustainability and reduces the need for continued involvement. Examples include:
- **Reverse Mentoring**: If your ERG has implemented reverse mentoring in the past, the priority now should be embedding it into the organisation's standard learning & development processes, owned by the Head of L&D, so the ERG doesn't need to stay involved.
- **Recruitment Campaigns**: Work with Talent Acquisition to establish a BAU process for involving diverse teams in recruitment efforts.

This approach should not draw on the time of the ERG leadership but should be done in a way that still highlights the benefits of ERGs to potential new joiners.

- **Pay and Promotion Processes**: Pay and promotion decisions directly influence pay equity and representation at senior levels. Depending on the data, useful practices might include:
  - Establishing Independent Observers for performance appraisal calibration or promotion discussions to ensure decisions are objective and evidence-based.
  - Conducting a pay audit to analyse micro-decisions on pay and bonuses, helping to identify and minimise inequities.

By balancing tactical (one-off) and strategic (sustainable and embedded) activities over the year, you ensure your ERG delivers immediate value while laying the groundwork for sustainable change.

If you are a large ERG with local Chapters, encourage your chapter leaders to apply the same principles to their planning.

## Create Balance

- Plan in Advance: Start each quarter by mapping out your activities by week. This will help you stay on track.
- Periodic Review: At the end of each week, month and quarter, check where you are against the plan, evaluate what worked, what didn't and why. Tweak your plan for the next period.

## Burnout Busting Tip

Ask yourself, "If I could only do one thing this quarter, what would have the biggest impact?" Use this as your anchor when building your balanced plan.

## *Everyday Inspo: Prioritise One Event*

*The ERG Leader for the Parents and Carers Network at a UK Marketing & Communication company, shared a powerful example of how focusing on one hero event per year can reduce workload while maximising impact. At the firm, each ERG receives hands-on support from the Comms and Marketing teams to deliver their flagship event.*

*For the Parents and Carers Network, this meant they could focus their energy on planning and delivering a standout event that truly resonated with their members and the broader organisation. With Comms and Marketing taking the lead on promotion, logistics, and creative assets, the burden on the ERG leadership team was significantly reduced, allowing them to concentrate on the content and member engagement.*

### *Key Takeaway*

*Collaborating with internal departments to deliver one hero event each year not only reduces the strain on ERG leaders but ensures the event has a professional, high-impact execution. It's a win-win strategy that engages members, demonstrates value to the organisation, and supports the ERG's quarterly priorities.*

# 3. Delegation

*"You can do anything, but not everything." David Allen*

Effective delegation is the cornerstone of sustainable ERG leadership. It's tempting to try and do everything yourself—after all, no one understands your vision for the network better than you, especially if you are the founder. But the reality is, wearing every hat is a one-way ticket to burnout. Sharing responsibilities doesn't just lighten your load; it empowers others, builds a stronger team, and creates space for you to focus on the bigger picture.

## The Importance of Structure

A clear structure is essential for effective delegation. Without it, roles and responsibilities can become muddled, especially in smaller networks, where the number of members is low e.g. 20 or less. In these networks, it's common to see all members attend planning meetings, with many remaining silent observers. Having specific set roles such as 'Comms lead' or 'Events and marketing' *can* work in some organisations but it can also be a barrier as volunteers may feel they don't have time to commit to extra work ongoing. These traditional roles can also lead to an over-emphasis on events at the expense of lasting change. Roles and responsibilities should be set in the context of the plan for the year and the quarterly priorities.

## 1. Leadership (Co-Chairs)

Have more than one co-chair (ideally 2–3 leaders) to share the workload and provide coverage during busy periods. This ensures no single person bears the full weight of responsibility.

## 2. Committee or Core Leadership Team

Form a small leadership team or committee of no more than 5–10 people, depending on the size and complexity of the organisation. In large, global organisations with regional chapters, this number may go up to 15. This is your core team of doers—the people who actively drive initiatives. Be clear with committee members that their role involves not only generating ideas but also rolling up their sleeves to deliver the quarterly priority.

## 3. General Membership

Have a clear definition and delineation for the broader membership group e.g. members sign up via a Microsoft or Google form, subscribe to a news feed, or join an internal online community. Their primary role is to contribute to building community, providing support, information, and advice to one another. Enable this group with the right system of processes, and tools. For example, if your company uses Microsoft:
- Use Microsoft Teams (Channel or SharePoint) for the leadership team or committee
- Use Viva Engage for the broader community to converse and connect.

# How to Delegate Effectively

## 1. Play to Strengths

Identify individuals who are capable and willing to contribute actively. Consider their strengths, interests, and availability. For example:
- Someone who is good at the detail could handle event logistics.
- A skilled communicator could liaise with Internal Comms on social media and the Intranet.
- A big picture thinker could help with process redesign.

## 2. Be Clear About Expectations

Provide clear instructions, including the purpose, scope, and desired outcome of each task or priority. Use tools like shared documents and project charters to keep everyone aligned.

## 3. Provide Support, Not Micromanagement

Check progress against milestones and key dates at the monthly planning meetings so you can offer guidance and troubleshoot issues, but avoid hovering over every detail. This fosters trust and allows team members to take ownership of their roles.

## 4. Don't Sweat the Small Stuff

As an ERG leader, your primary focus should be on the quarterly priorities. If a lower-priority initiative, like a fireside chat, starts to go off track, use your monthly planning meetings to monitor progress, provide support, and give assistance on the process where needed.

However, resist the temptation to dive in and redirect your attention from the agreed priorities. Remember, there's only one of you. Once the quarterly priorities are set, avoid adding additional tasks to your to-do list otherwise this will lead to burnout.

Your role as a leader is to focus on the bigger picture not to put out every tiny fire.

## Tools and Techniques

- Checklists and Templates: Standardised templates for recurring tasks, like event planning or process reviews with clear milestones, timescales, approach and sign off points save time and make it easier to monitor progress
- Regular Check-ins: Monthly meetings help maintain momentum and address challenges early.

---

## Create Balance

- Establish a clear ERG structure, a core committee of doers, and a supportive community that understands their role.
- When ideas are proposed by members, encourage them to take the lead to foster ownership and shared responsibility.
- Focus your energy on the quarterly priority and resist the urge to overextend by diving into low-priority initiatives.

## Burnout Busting Tip

Delegation isn't a one-time event—it's a skill you develop over time. Start small, celebrate successes, and gradually expand the scope of what you delegate.

# *Everyday Inspo: Encouraging Ownership Through Delegation*

*The leader of the Multicultural ERG at a large UK Utility and an alumnus of my ERG Complete Leader training course, has a no-nonsense approach to delegation and fostering a team of doers.*

*When committee members bring an idea to the network they are encouraged to take full ownership and lead the initiative, with the requisite support. This ensures that the committee doesn't operate as a group of idea generators but as an active team committed to delivering on their ideas.*

*By empowering members to lead their own projects, she creates a culture of shared responsibility and engagement. This approach not only lightens the workload for ERG leaders but also enhances the sense of ownership and achievement within the committee.*

## *Key Takeaway*

*Encouraging committee members to take ownership of their ideas fosters a team of doers and builds accountability. It's a practical way to drive engagement and ensure the workload is distributed fairly across the network.*

Balanced: The Little Book of Burnout-Free ERG Leadership

# 4. Time Management

*"Manage your time, manage your life."*

Time is the one resource that ERG leaders can't create more of, but managing it effectively can make all the difference between thriving and burning out. As a leader juggling network responsibilities, your day job, and personal commitments, it's easy to feel stretched to breaking point.

However, with the right strategies, you can take control of your time and make space for what truly matters.

## Focus on What Matters

Not all tasks are created equal. Identify the activities that align with your quarterly priorities and delegate or defer anything that doesn't directly contribute to these goals. This focus prevents you from getting bogged down in low-impact tasks.

## Time-Blocking

When I was in Finance and leading a team of Financial Planning & Analysis, our diaries were very much driven by the Finance Calendar for planning and reporting. Knowing when Board Meetings or Budget presentations were due to happen I would block out time for the preparation and submission of papers.

Then I would also block out time to prepare for the meeting itself, if I was presenting. Time-blocking is one of the simplest yet most powerful tools in your arsenal. By scheduling blocks of uninterrupted time for key activities—whether it's preparing for a meeting, doing focused work, brainstorming new ideas, or responding to emails—you can work more efficiently and reduce distractions. Protect these blocks as you would any important meeting.

## Set Boundaries

ERG responsibilities can creep into every hour if you allow it, leading to long hours to stay on top of the day job. Set clear boundaries for when and how you'll engage with network tasks. For example:

- Allocate specific times during the week for ERG work.

- Turn off notifications after-hours.
- Communicate your availability to your team and members so they know when to reach out—and when not.

Time management can be influenced by the business etiquette and culture of the organisation. Some companies encourage individuals to take breaks, like lunch(!) and schedule them into the calendar. Other companies routinely schedule meetings outside of working hours and expect employees to be available at all times. Setting boundaries in these long-hours cultures can be incredibly challenging but it is vital to maintaining balance.

## Leverage Technology

Make the most of tools that help you stay organised and efficient. Examples include:

- Project Management Software: Tools like Asana or Trello, or even Excel (if you want to keep it low-tech), can help you track tasks and deadlines.
- Calendars and Planners: Use a digital or physical planner to organise your day and prioritise tasks.
- Automation: automate repetitive tasks like email responses or calendar scheduling where possible, even using AI tools to help lighten the load.

## Managing Expectations with Your Manager

Time management isn't just about personal strategies—it also needs your line manager to be on board. Most organisations do not pay their ERG leaders for their work. In the US, an estimated 40% of ERG leaders receive compensation, while outside the US, the figure drops significantly to around 5%. However, some companies agree on an allocation of time, such as one day per month, that can be carved out specifically for ERG activities.

If you're a volunteer ERG leader in a high-pressure, long-hours culture with no formal agreement on time allocation, consider leveraging any existing policies around volunteering days. Many organisations encourage employees to take 3–5 days per year for community volunteering. Use this as a starting point to negotiate dedicated time for network responsibilities. Having this conversation early can help manage expectations and set clear boundaries, ensuring your ERG work doesn't come at the expense of your well-being or day job performance.

If you are finding it difficult to get agreement or buy-in from your line manager, seek support from your Executive Sponsor. This could take the form of advice in how to approach it with your manager and could extend to the Exec sponsor speaking to your manager on your behalf. This is a difficult situation to navigate so arm yourself with the facts e.g. how other ERG leaders in your firm are being supported, and proceed with caution.

## Create Balance

- Use time-blocking techniques to protect focus time for ERG work and avoid back-to-back meetings.
- Have an open conversation with your line manager and Exec Sponsor to set expectations about the time allocated for your ERG role.
- Monitor your organisation's culture for practices that might make time management harder, and set personal boundaries accordingly.

## Burnout Busting Tip

Remember, managing your time isn't about squeezing more into your day—it's about making intentional choices to focus on what matters most. A well-managed schedule leaves room for creativity, reflection, and, most importantly, rest.

# *Everyday Inspo: The Power of Firm Boundaries*

*The head of the Global Gender Network at a banking giant, is one busy ERG Leader. In addition to her senior role within the business, she teaches yoga, chairs a charity, and has a young family. Hearing her list of commitments, the question immediately springs to mind: How does she do it all?*

*The answer lies in her approach to boundaries. When I invited her to join me on my weekly LinkedIn Live which streams at 8.30a.m, she made it clear that early morning slots were a non-starter unless it was during school holidays, when she wasn't doing the school run. It meant waiting a bit longer to have her on the show, but it gave me a valuable insight into her strategy for managing time and avoiding over-commitment.*

*By setting firm boundaries, she ensures that her time is allocated to what matters most. Her approach demonstrates how ERG leaders can effectively manage demanding schedules without sacrificing their personal priorities or burning out.*

## *Key Takeaway*

*Firm boundaries are essential for managing time and avoiding over-commitment. By clearly defining what is and isn't negotiable, this leader exemplifies how others can successfully balance multiple roles while maintaining their well-being and effectiveness.*

Balanced: The Little Book of Burnout-Free ERG Leadership

# 5. Managing Emotional Labour

*"You can't pour from an empty cup."*

ERG leaders often become the go-to person for support, advice, and guidance within their networks. While this role can be incredibly rewarding, it also comes with a unique set of challenges. The emotional labour involved in supporting members, navigating sensitive topics, and advocating for change can take a significant toll on your mental and emotional well-being if not managed carefully.

## Set Clear Boundaries

It's easy to become the unofficial therapist, counsellor, union rep, or even line manager for your network members, but it's neither sustainable nor healthy. Remind yourself and your members that your role is to lead and enable the network, not to solve everyone's problems. Do this instead:

- Signpost Resources: Direct members to appropriate support channels such as Employee Assistance Programmes (EAPs), HR reporting processes, or external resources.
- Build the Community: Encourage members to support one another through events, online forums, or informal connections, reducing the reliance on you as an individual.
- Stay in Your Lane: Avoid taking on roles you aren't equipped for, such as providing legal advice or counselling.

If the support mechanisms such as EAPs or online community forums, are inadequate, tackle it as a quarterly priority.

# The Emotional Toil of Fighting for Social Justice

Many ERG leaders describe their work as feeling like a constant battle. Advocating for social justice and inclusion, especially in organisations where managers or leaders are not fully bought in, can be exhausting. This emotional toll is compounded by the slow pace of change and the resistance that leaders often face.

There is a pragmatic need to pick your battles wisely. Focus on areas where you can make the greatest impact and align your efforts with organisational priorities to maximise buy-in. Additionally, lean on your Exec Sponsor for perspective and support. Be open about your stress and concerns, and use them as a sounding board to help you navigate difficult situations. Their role is not just to champion the ERG but to help you stay grounded and resilient.

## Enable Community Support

Creating a culture of peer support within your ERG can alleviate the pressure on leaders. Use tools like Viva Engage, Slack or Discord to establish online forums where members can share experiences, ask questions, and provide advice to one another. Encourage open dialogue and collaboration to foster a sense of shared responsibility. Become like the website *Mumsnet,* but for employee networks.

## Mental Health First Aid (MHFA) and Supervision

Consider mental health first aid training for you and members of the ERG leadership team. This training provides valuable tools to recognise signs of distress and offer initial support without overstepping boundaries. Additionally, regular supervision or check-ins with specialist MHFA organisations can help monitor your well-being as Leaders, allow you the space to reflect on the emotional challenges of your role and keep burnout at bay.

## Self-Care Strategies

There is a wealth of resources available on self-care strategies, and rather than attempting to list them out here I would encourage leaders to figure out what works best for them. However, some of my favourite strategies include:

- Journalling: Writing down thoughts and feelings can help process emotions and identify stress triggers.
- Scheduling Personal Time: Put time in your diary for activities you love—daily or weekly. Whether it's reading, exercising, singing or spending time with loved ones, make it a non-negotiable part of your calendar.
- Taking Regular Holidays: Avoid leaving all your annual leave to take in one period; instead, take regular breaks throughout the year to recharge.

Pay attention to the signs that your stress levels are rising. Do you become short-tempered, easily irritated, or forgetful? Do you swear (curse) more often? Recognising these early warning signs allows you to create a plan for how to address them before they escalate. Whether it's stepping back, seeking support, or prioritising rest, having a strategy in place is key.

---

## Create Balance

- Build a supportive ERG community where members can connect with and support each other.
- Set boundaries and signpost members to appropriate resources, like the company's EAP, to ensure the burden isn't on you.
- Watch for signs of rising stress levels in yourself, and have a plan to address them before they escalate.

## Burnout Busting Tip

Remember, you're not the ERG. The strength of the network lies in its members and the collective community you build—not in how much you personally shoulder. Prioritise your well-being so you can continue to lead effectively.

## *Everyday Inspo: Defining 'Support'*

*During an in-house workshop with an organisation that championed friendship and support as foundational pillars of the ERGs, a key challenge emerged: this principle was being applied inconsistently across the networks and people were unclear what it meant.*

*In some networks, leaders had become informal points of contact for employees facing personal and professional challenges. These leaders found themselves taking on roles that extended far beyond their remit, sometimes because the organisation's Employee Assistance Programmes (EAPs) were perceived as under-resourced and inadequate.*

*In contrast, other networks had set clear boundaries. These ERG leaders listened to members' concerns but firmly directed them to appropriate support channels, such as HR or external resources. This approach not only ensured employees received the specialised help they needed but also protected the leaders from bearing undue emotional labour.*

### *Key Takeaway*

*A principle like "friendship and support" can mean different things in practice, but ERGs must establish boundaries to avoid burnout. Leaders should focus on creating a supportive culture where members feel heard while signposting them to appropriate resources for deeper assistance. Clear boundaries ensure the ERG remains a safe space without overburdening its leaders.*

Balanced: The Little Book of Burnout-Free ERG Leadership

# 6. Support Networks

*"If you want to go fast, go alone. If you want to go far, go with others." African Proverb*

No ERG leader is an island. Building a strong support network is essential to sustaining your leadership, maintaining balance, and amplifying the impact of your ERG.

Many ERG leaders have shared that they often feel like lone warriors, fighting battles in isolation. A robust support network can help tackle that feeling of loneliness and provide the encouragement and resources you need to succeed.

## Key Support Pillars

### 1. Your Sponsor

Your Exec Sponsor plays a critical role in your success. Schedule regular one-to-ones monthly to update them on progress, discuss challenges, and seek advice. In addition to these regular catch-ups, your sponsor should also attend the leadership or committee planning meetings once every quarter. This provides an opportunity for them to give feedback and support on the quarterly priorities and ensures alignment between the ERG and organisational goals.

## 2. Your Line Manager

Your line manager is another vital source of support. Having an open conversation about your ERG responsibilities and how they align with your day job can help set realistic expectations and gain their backing. Their support is especially important in managing your time and ensuring your ERG commitments are recognised as part of your overall contribution to the organisation.

## 3. HR and DEI Champions

Build collaborative relationships with HR and DEI teams. The ERGs role is ten times more stressful if you are not working hand in glove with HR and DEI.

These departments can be invaluable allies, aligning your ERG's efforts with broader people and culture strategies. Partner with them to address systemic issues, access employee data, and amplify your initiatives.

## 4. Peer Support

Connect with other ERG leaders, both within your organisation and externally. Peer networks provide a safe space to share challenges, exchange ideas, and learn from others' experiences. Many leaders find these connections to be some of their most valuable sources of support.

## 5. Mentors and Coaches

Seek out mentors or professional coaches to guide your personal and professional growth. These relationships can help you develop skills, set boundaries, and navigate tricky situations with confidence.

## 6. Your Community

Don't forget about the members of your ERG! They can be a source of inspiration, encouragement, and insight. Foster a sense of ownership within the community by encouraging members to share their feedback and take an active role in shaping the network.

# Leveraging External Networks

Beyond your immediate environment, external networks can help to inspire and re-energise. Consider joining industry groups, attending ERG summits like the ERG Leader Summit, or collaborating with ERG leaders in other organisations.

External partnerships can provide fresh perspectives, resources, and ideas while reducing your workload through shared initiatives. Additionally, explore "networks of networks"—platforms that bring together ERG leaders across industries—which can be invaluable sources of support and information. We'll list some of these in the Resources section.

---

## Create Balance

- Check In Regularly: Schedule consistent check-ins with your sponsor, line manager, and other key stakeholders to stay aligned and supported.
- Ask for Help: Don't hesitate to reach out when you're feeling overwhelmed—your network is there to support you.
- Expand Your Horizons: Attend workshops, webinars, or conferences to grow your skills and broaden your perspective.

## Burnout Busting Tip

Your support network isn't just a safety net—it's a launchpad. Regularly engage with your sponsor, peers, and external networks to share challenges, celebrate successes, and spark new ideas. Lean on others to remind yourself that you're never in this alone.

## *Everyday Inspo: Building Community Through the ERG Leader Summit*

*In 2024, network leaders from across the UK came together for the ERG Leader Summit, creating a unique space for connection, learning, and support. The event brought together individuals facing similar challenges, enabling them to share experiences, exchange ideas, and find practical solutions to common problems.*

*The Summit didn't just provide value during the event—it fostered a sense of community that extended far beyond the day itself. Attendees continued to collaborate and support one another, building networks of networks that strengthened their ERGs. The event also introduced participants to experts and service providers who could offer specialised guidance, from data analytics to event management.*

### *Key Takeaway*

*External networking events like the ERG Leader Summit provide a great opportunity for ERG leaders to connect with peers, build lasting relationships, and access expert resources. These events are beneficial for personal growth, professional support, and organisational impact.*

# 7. Navigating Conflict and Controversy

*"He who knows only his own side of the case knows little of that." John Stuart Mill*

Conflict and controversy are common when leading an ERG, particularly when tackling sensitive topics or advocating for systemic change. From navigating internal disagreements to responding to external events in a social-media enabled world, ERG leaders must be prepared to handle these situations with care, diplomacy, and strategic thinking.

## Internal Conflicts: Power Struggles and Role Creep

Internal conflicts often arise from power struggles within the ERG. For some members, the network provides a rare sense of validation, especially if they feel unfulfilled in their day jobs. This can lead to overreach, with individuals seeking greater influence or visibility. Ways to tackle this include:

- Have open conversations to align strengths with roles and responsibilities.

- Ensure work is fairly distributed, and create opportunities for everyone to contribute meaningfully.

- Reinforce that the ERG is a team effort and there's more than enough work to go around.

# External Controversies: Geopolitical and Social Justice Issues

Individuals often turn to ERG leaders in times of crisis or when looking for the company to respond to major events. These might include:

- Identity-based hate crimes or protests widely covered in the media

- Wars, elections, or geopolitical crises.

Such events can trigger heightened emotions from members and raise practical concerns, such as physical safety, or a desire to understand the organisation's stance on the issue.

- Emotional Support: Organise listening circles or safe spaces for members to share their experiences. Where possible, engage trained facilitators to run these sessions, ideally funded through the employee wellbeing budget.

- Position Statements: If members push for a public statement from the organisation, work with HR, Comms, and your Exec Sponsor to navigate this carefully. Not every issue will result in a position statement; the decision should align with the organisation's policies, values, and the severity of the issue.

# Tricky Conversations: Navigating Conflict-Avoidant Cultures

In conflict-avoidant cultures, like the UK, addressing disagreements or controversial topics can feel particularly challenging. ERG leaders need to:

- Preface conversations with statements like, "This might be a difficult conversation," to set expectations.
- Focus on evidence-based discussions and the shared goals of the network and organisation.

- Seek external advice or insights from other ERG leaders to approach sensitive topics effectively.

## Tools for Managing Conflict

- Build Trust: Establish trust with the ERG community and stakeholders by being transparent, empathetic, and consistent.
- Set Ground Rules: Establish norms for respectful communication in person and online, during meetings and discussions.
- Document Decisions: Maintain clear records of decisions and actions to ensure accountability and avoid misunderstandings.

### Create Balance

- Pick Your Battles: Focus your energy on issues where you can make the most meaningful impact.
- Lean on Your Sponsor: Use your Exec Sponsor as a sounding board when navigating particularly tricky situations.
- Learn from Others: Reach out to ERG leaders internally or externally for advice and insights on managing similar challenges.

## Burnout Busting Tip

Not every conflict needs to be solved immediately. Take a step back and assess the bigger picture. Address issues with empathy and clarity, and remember that building trust and unity takes time. Rely on your sponsor and stakeholders to help manage tensions effectively.

# *Everyday Inspo: Navigating Controversy with Sensitivity*

*The most recent Israel-Gaza conflict presented one of the most contentious and emotive challenges for ERGs to navigate. In one organisation, a large global law firm, ERGs were deeply moved by the human suffering and wanted to respond with a message of support and solidarity.*

*Recognising the complexity and sensitivity of the issue, the ERGs collaborated with the Head of People and Culture to craft a response that was respectful to all communities affected. Together, they ensured the internal message focused on universal themes of compassion and human suffering while avoiding language that might inadvertently alienate or upset others.*

*This collaborative approach allowed the organisation to acknowledge the pain experienced by its employees and external communities without exacerbating tensions or divisions.*

## *Key Takeaway*

*When responding to geopolitical or social justice issues, collaboration with senior leadership is crucial to ensure messaging is sensitive, balanced, and inclusive. By focusing on shared values and seeking input from key stakeholders, ERGs can provide support in a way that unites rather than divides.*

Balanced: The Little Book of Burnout-Free ERG Leadership

# 8. Operating Politically and Strategically

*"The key to leadership is influence, not authority."*
*Ken Blanchard*

Many ERG leaders come from a place of passion—driven by a deep commitment to doing the right thing, a sense of fairness, and a desire to help others. While this passion is a powerful motivator, when unleashed without focus, it can sometimes hinder effective influencing. In some cases, it may even lead to others feeling put off or less supportive of the network.

Passion alone isn't usually enough to have a lasting impact. Navigating organisational dynamics with political and strategic acumen is essential for building influence, getting access to resources, and embedding initiatives into BAU (Business As Usual). While "politics" may carry a negative connotation, operating politically doesn't mean being manipulative—it means being intentional, ethical, and strategic in how you influence others and achieve your goals.

# Map Your Senior Stakeholders

## 1. Map Your Network

Identify key stakeholders including HR, the DEI team, and Senior Leaders beyond your Exec Sponsor. Who has the influence to help your ERG succeed? It is important to identify individuals who are influential allies and very supportive, as well as those who are not necessarily allies. If there are individuals who are not as supportive, work with your sponsor to engage them, build trusting relationships, and get their feedback on what the ERG could do to be more beneficial to their area of the organisation.

## 2. Understand Their Priorities:

Understand what matters to each stakeholder and their area of business. Are they focused on innovation, talent retention, compliance, customer service? Align your messaging with their priorities to gain their support.

## 3. High-Influence Allies

Build strong bonds with influential allies, including those who may not immediately seem supportive of your goals. Regularly meet with them (every 3–6 months) to share updates, seek feedback, and remove obstacles. Look for ways to involve them in delivering one of the quarterly priorities.

## Pick Your Moments

Advocating for change requires timing and tact. Avoid pushing too hard or fast on issues that lack organisational readiness and stakeholder support. Instead:

- Remind People of Previous Wins: Share stories of the network's past successes and individual member stories to build credibility and demonstrate impact.
- Introduce Ideas Gradually: Introduce complex or controversial ideas over time, framing them in terms of the benefits to individuals and their areas of responsibility.
- Link to Broader Goals: Work out how your quarterly priorities can be directly linked to company objectives, priorities, or external partner events. This approach increases engagement and secures senior leader support.

## Leverage Evidence and Data

Influence is much stronger when it's backed by evidence. Use employee survey results, engagement metrics, or case studies to make your case. Data helps you move from opinions to facts, making it easier for stakeholders to see the value of your initiatives.

## Strategic Communication

- Tailor Your Messaging: Adjust your language and tone based on your audience. For senior leaders, focus on concise, results-oriented messaging that demonstrates how the network helps to deliver company goals.
- Present Solutions, Not Just Problems: When addressing challenges, frame them in terms of actionable solutions. Highlight how your ERG is not just identifying issues but actively driving meaningful change that benefits the organisation as a whole.
- Keep it Simple and Focused: Confused people don't buy, so clarity is key. Prioritise the most important points and avoid overwhelming senior leaders with excessive details or jargon. Be very clear about what you need them to know and what they need to do about it.
- Stories of Success: Be armed and ready with success stories from your members and beyond that demonstrates the benefit that the network brings - think of it as part of your elevator pitch.

# Avoid Common Pitfalls

- Overloading the Agenda: Don't try to fix everything at once. This is why having one priority per quarter is useful. Show how your quarterly goals align with organisation and stakeholder priorities.
- Burnout from 'Drum-Banging': Understand that not every battle can be fought at the same time. Focus on areas where your energy will have the greatest impact.
- Undermining Relationships: Even when disagreements arise, maintain professionalism and a collaborative mindset to preserve long-term relationships.

## Create Balance

- Meet Regularly: Schedule regular catch ups with key stakeholders to share progress and seek input.
- Seek Feedback: Actively ask for constructive feedback to flex your approach and build trust.
- Learn the Politics: Observe organisational dynamics and learn from those who are good at navigating them effectively.

## Burnout Busting Tip

Strategy isn't about doing more; it's about doing what matters most. Focus your energy where it will have the greatest impact, and don't be afraid to say no to distractions. Ask yourself, am I being strategic about my efforts, or am I spreading myself too thin by tackling too many challenges at once?

## *Everyday Inspo: A Perfect Collaboration Between ERG and Business Strategy*

*The Chair of the Race, Ethnicity, and Cultural Heritage (REACH) network at a leading car manufacturer, led a truly groundbreaking initiative that balanced fundraising, member development, and alignment with the company's strategic imperatives.*

*The project began with a collaboration between the REACH network and The Washing Machine Project, which develops sustainable, no-power washing machines. The network brought the idea to the company's engineers, who took the concept design and turned the machines into reality.*

*The network leader focused on supporting members through unique experiences, taking a cohort of women from diverse cultural backgrounds on a walking expedition in Scotland, which included cold-water swimming. This was a life-changing opportunity for personal and professional growth and connection. To cap it off, the group travelled in company vehicles, showcasing the business's commitment to its people and its brand.*

*Through these and similar endeavours, the network raised funds to deliver the 10 machines to Diepsloot, a township in South Africa. The machines were presented to the local community by the REACH network leader alongside the senior leadership team in the region, symbolising a tangible commitment to sustainability and community development.*

*This initiative garnered wide support, external PR and collaboration across the firm, illustrating how ERGs can successfully align their activities with both individual member development and organisational objectives.*

## *Key Takeaway*

*The REACH network's collaboration with The Washing Machine Project is a model for impactful ERG initiatives. By supporting individual growth, fostering collaboration, and aligning with the company's strategic focus on sustainability, this project showcased the power of ERGs to create value for both their members and the broader business.*

# 9. Celebrating Wins

*"Proud moments are the building blocks of confidence and self-belief." Deepak Chopra*

Celebrating wins is not just about recognising success —it's about harnessing the energising impact of progress. For ERG leaders, it can be a powerful reminder that you are making a difference, even when the challenges feel overwhelming. Celebrating wins can combat the urge to strive for perfectionism or add more tasks to your plate in an endless pursuit of success. Sometimes, recognising the progress you've made is the key to sustaining momentum and preventing burnout.

## Why Celebrate Wins?

- Reinforce Progress: Celebrating accomplishments, big or small, helps you see how far the ERG has come, reminding you and your team that your efforts are paying off.

- Motivate and Energise: Acknowledging successes boosts morale and creates positive energy for future initiatives.
- Build Credibility: Sharing wins with stakeholders demonstrates the value of the ERG and strengthens support for your work.

## How to Celebrate Wins

- Shoutouts and Recognition: Publicly acknowledge team members' contributions in meetings, emails, or on social media. A simple "thank you" can go a long way in making people feel appreciated.
- Event Highlights: Share stories and outcomes from events on internal and external platforms, showcasing how they made an impact on the community or the organisation.
- Annual Highlights: Compile a short summary of the year's achievements, including key milestones and memorable moments, to share with stakeholders.
- Collaborative Wins: Work with stakeholders, such as HR or Internal Comms, to highlight ERG contributions in broader organisational communications such as newsletters and intranet pages.

## Progress, Not Perfection

Celebrating wins isn't about waiting for perfection; it's about recognising effort and progress. Progress is the real measure of success, and even small steps forward contribute to meaningful change. Remember:

- Avoid the Overload: Resist the temptation to add more tasks or goals just to achieve a bigger win. Your existing efforts are enough.
- Highlight What's Working: Celebrate the initiatives that are making a difference, even if they're not fully complete or perfect.
- Take Time to Reflect: Use celebrations as a moment to pause, reflect, and recharge before moving on to the next challenge.

---

## Create Balance

- Celebrate Small and Often: Don't wait for the end of the year—acknowledge wins at the end of every quarter, or even at the end of every monthly meeting.
- Share the Joy: Involve your team, members, and stakeholders in celebrations to spread positivity.

- Use Visuals: Highlight wins with photos, videos, or infographics of key stats to make the impact more tangible and memorable.

## Burnout Busting Tip

Celebrating isn't just for the big moments. Take time to acknowledge incremental progress—every step forward is worth recognising. Ask yourself, am I recognising progress, or am I focusing too much on what still needs to be done?

## *Everyday Inspo: Celebrating Wins Through Awards*

*A UK Building Society's Black Network achieved a remarkable milestone when they entered and won the UK's Black Talent Award for Employee Network of the Year. Despite being a relatively new network, they were able to demonstrate a tangible impact within just a few years, earning recognition for their achievements.*

*Winning such an award is not only a testament to the network's hard work but also a memorable and meaningful way to celebrate success. Award ceremonies provide a powerful platform to showcase achievements, build credibility, and boost morale. However, celebrating wins doesn't always need to be on such a grand scale. A simple post on Viva Engage (internal) or LinkedIn can also be an effective way to recognise and share progress.*

## *Key Takeaway*

*Celebrating wins is essential to sustaining momentum and energy levels within an ERG. Whether it's winning an award, posting on internal platforms, or sharing achievements on LinkedIn, finding ways to regularly highlight success reinforces the value of the network. Quarterly celebrations can help maintain focus, motivate members, and ensure the network's progress remains visible.*

# 10. Leveraging External Resources and Communities

*"Think like there is no box."*

ERG leaders don't have to do it all alone. By tapping into external resources and communities, you can amplify your impact, reduce your workload, and bring fresh ideas and expertise into your organisation. Collaboration and knowledge-sharing beyond your organisation's walls send a strong message to senior leaders: your ERG understands the value of unity and external partnerships, which can be a game-changer for building support and credibility.

## Key Areas

### Data and Metrics

Having access to reliable data is crucial for making sure you are focusing on the right things. It reduces the risk of being 'busy fools'. Here's how you can leverage available data resources:

### 1. Internal Data

Start by working with your employee survey provider and HR data teams to gather internal data that reflects the experiences and needs of your network members.

### 2. External Resources

Consider organisations like The Equal Group, Flair, and DIAL—leaders in the field of diversity, equity, and inclusion (DEI) data and analysis. These organisations offer valuable insights and benchmarks to guide your strategy. They can also audit your policies, giving you ideas for which ones should be reviewed.

## Reverse Mentoring

Reverse mentoring is commonly used by ERGs and can be a powerful tool for fostering inclusivity and mutual understanding within your organisation when implemented correctly AND when senior leaders are on board.

Patrice Gordon's Book, *Reverse Mentoring: Removing Barriers and Building Belonging in the Workplace,* has become the go-to resource, sharing her experience and offering practical guidance on how to implement and sustain reverse mentoring programs.

## Development Programs

When it comes to leadership development, ERG leaders should act as the bridge between their network's needs and the expertise available within the organisation rather than being the de facto delivery of training, which brings risks (unless suitably qualified) and extra workload.

- Work with L&D (Learning and Development) teams to bring in external partners who can tailor development programs to the specific needs of your network.
- As the ERG leader, you can help to coordinate these efforts at the start, and ensure L&D understands the community's needs, but let the experts handle the heavy lifting. This approach shifts the workload to where it should be.

## Event Management

Events are a key part of ERG engagement, but they can be time-consuming and workload-heavy.

## 1. Flagship Events:

For major events, such as International Women's Day or Pride Month, agree with your internal or external Comms and events teams that they will do the heavy lifting. These teams should take the lead on logistics to reduce the burden on you.

## 2. Planning Tools:

For other events, consider customising standard event planning checklists e.g. from websites like Eventbrite, to guide through the process step-by-step. Add internal approvals, processes and typical timescales. This checklist can be used by anyone in the leadership team or committee so they can take the pressure off you as the leader.

## 3. Collaborations with Other ERGs:

- Collaborating with other ERGs can help you share the workload, especially for community-building networking events.
- For example, consider collaborating with 4 organisations to host a quarterly event. Each network hosts an event at their location, but each network only has to organise one event, reducing the workload significantly but delivering 4 superb events for their members.

### 4. Event Planning Platforms:

Websites like Togather in the UK allow you to input your event requirements and receive quotes, streamlining the process of finding event suppliers. This can help reduce stress and ensure quality events with minimal effort.

## Pay and Promotion Processes

These processes often sit at the heart of addressing inequity and senior level representation but their opacity and confidentiality can make it both difficult and frustrating to embed sustainable change. This why external support can be invaluable in these areas. For example:

- Pay Audits: Collaborate with HR to engage external consultants that can analyse the micro-decisions on pay and bonuses that lead to pay gaps and pay inequality. Agree with HR that this becomes a regular process which is undertaken at least every 2-3 years.
- Independent Observers: Work with HR to standardise the addition of individuals who are tasked with challenging objectivity in performance calibration and promotion discussions.
- Select & Assess: Work with Talent Acquisition and HR to ensure a diverse mix of employees is used in recruitment campaigns, interview and selection panels in a way that doesn't overburden ERG leaders.

# External Networks

The rise of 'networks of networks'—groups that connect ERG leaders across industries—offers a wealth of support and inspiration. Joining these groups allows you to learn from others, share resources, and build collaborations that amplify your efforts. Conferences and summits, in person and online events can also be a source of external support.

---

## Create Balance

- Start Small: Don't feel the need to adopt every external resource at once. Choose one or two that will instantly reduce workload and help you deliver the quarterly priorities more efficiently.
- Collaborate Creatively: Shared events or cross-organisational initiatives can ease your workload and introduce fresh perspectives.
- Keep Learning: Attend conferences, summits, and webinars to stay inspired and connected.

### Burnout Busting Tip

Collaboration is king. Don't hesitate to tap into external expertise, whether it's partnering with charities, joining cross-industry networks, or consulting with DEI professionals. Am I making the most of external expertise, or am I trying to do everything using the 'same old' internal methods?

# *Everyday Inspo: The Power of External Support*

*When the idea was floated to launch a men's network at a global Facilities Management provider, they wanted to ensure it would be both relevant and impactful for its members. Recognising that setting up an ERG from scratch comes with challenges, the leader sought external support to guide the process.*

*He reached out to Andy's Man Club, a renowned organisation supporting men's mental health, to help shape the network's purpose and generate ideas for activities and initiatives. This external collaboration provided valuable insights and a framework to ensure the network started off on the right foot. By leveraging the expertise of an established group, they were able to build a network that resonated deeply with members and aligned with a clear mission.*

## *Key Takeaway:*

*Seeking external expertise can be invaluable when establishing or evolving an ERG. By collaborating with organisations like Andy's Man Club, networks can draw on proven strategies and fresh ideas to create initiatives that are both meaningful and impactful.*

Leveraging External Resources and Communities

Balanced: The Little Book of Burnout-Free ERG Leadership

# Final Thoughts: Creating Balance

I recently heard the quote, "*It's not about finding balance, it's about creating it.*" I couldn't agree more.

As an ERG leader, you're already making a difference—not just for your network but for your entire organisation. This work can be transformative, but it can also be overwhelming if not approached with balance and intention. The role demands vision, resilience, and strategic thinking, but above all, it requires you to prioritise your well-being.

The key takeaway from this book is simple yet powerful: You don't have to do it all. Progress, not perfection, is what truly drives meaningful change. By focusing on clear priorities, building strong support systems, and leveraging resources strategically, you can lead with impact while avoiding burnout.

Remember, balance is not a static state—it's a daily practice. There will be times when the plates you're spinning wobble, and that's okay. The strength of an ERG lies not in any single individual but in the collective power of its members, allies, and supporters.

Lean on them, celebrate the wins, and don't be afraid to step back when needed to recharge.

Finally, know that you are part of a larger movement. You're paving the way for a fairer, happier, more fulfilling workplace. Your leadership matters, and the ripples of your work will extend far beyond what you can see today.

Thank you for taking on this important role. I hope this book has provided practical tools, inspiration, and reassurance that you are enough, just as you are.

Keep leading, keep learning, and keep striving for balance.

You've got this.

www.ingramcontent.com/pod-product-compliance
Lightning Source LLC
Chambersburg PA
CBHW070347230526
45471CB00006B/2455